How to Extricate

Laura Theis

How to Extricate Yourself

©Laura Theis

First Edition 2020

Laura Theis has asserted her authorship and given her permission to
Dempsey & Windle for these poems to be published here.

Published by Dempsey & Windle
15 Rosetrees
Guildford
Surrey
GU1 2HS
UK
01483 571164
dempseyandwindle.com

British Library Cataloguing-in-Publication Data

A catalogue record for this book is available from the British Library

ISBN: 978-1-913329-36-5

Cover art by Laura Theis

Printed by Imprint Digital, Exeter, UK

for Mascha Kaléko

Contents

How to Extricate Yourself   7

I   FALSE ADVERTISING

insomnia   9
writer in residence   10
Rain and Deception   12
it's never one of the good ones   13
The Clockmaker's Daughter   14
Sehnsucht   15
purple sea   16
zombie apocalypse self-knowledge   17
concerning things which turn out to have an unexpected application
wholly different from their intended use   18
false advertising   19

II   A FLIGHT OF FAMILIARS

Initiation   21
Colour of the Witch   22
familiar   24
Medusae   25
for soft long ears   26
Storm Petrel   27
tiny choirboy   28
advice from one who's been burnt before   29
Saying Goodbye to Wychwood   30
Aurae   32
Raising Astaroth   33
anemochory   34
aftermath   35

III   HOSTINGHOSTING

prediction   37
What It Felt Like   38
adaptation   40
On Working In A Shop   41
what we know   42
but the dancer   44
to the man who told me my yellow bobble hat makes me look old   45
There's A Tyre Swing In Bagley Wood   46
hostinghosting   48
salt apples   50

Acknowledgments   51
About Laura Theis   54

How to Extricate Yourself

Here, balancing precariously, scared to bend your knees,
while the naughty children ignore the neurotic poetry recital.
(The next round will be symbolically dry
but for now the wine clinks pleasantly in the glasses.)

Or with some birds in the chalky mist, displaying
jewels you wish you will never own.
Or in the syrupy night. Or sweating.
Or vulnerable, happy, singing, saying yes to everything.

Or saying things out loud in the light.
Or crying, or clutching your lucky key,
like those scenes from a dream factory.

Or just in a whirl of old colours, raspberries in May.
Amber, petrol. Wrapped candy.
A young girl on a horse in a shower of smiles, cradling nothing.

I FALSE ADVERTISING

insomnia

past midnight with my eyes shut
      it gets easier
      to believe

I am a white-winged bird
      not a woman half in love
      with unrequited sleep

writer in residence

look up: here I am my love
can you see me waving?
no of course not all you see is
a pale oval in your sky
but remember it's the only map
you need to find me now

I write to you at least I try
black ink on moonstone
white chalk on lunar rock
it's not going well today
the writing
I keep looking down

I think of you but seeing our old home's glow
blue and calm
my thoughts drift to your astronaut wife and how
you left her for my sake though maybe she's the one
who knew how to leave you already
having had all this practice in rockets and ships

and what I am wondering is whether
maybe it was because she loved
each minuscule piece of stardust
a little bit more than you?
forgive me you never wanted to be left behind
like a satellite again

I know you thought you would be safe
with me safe from all the heartache and I'm sorry
I'm trying to make sense of my coming here
I'm trying to make sense of how tides work
did you know we used to explain lunacy with the idea
that our brains are mostly water?

did you know that since I'm the first writer in residence
there is no library here yet?
I could only find the driest reading materials – manuals and such
except one beautiful book about the cosmos
but I can't recommend it
to readers who don't like to be reminded of their irrelevance

yesterday I finished a chapter on the timeline of our future
now I know that 5 billion years from now the sun will expand
and expand
until it has dwarfed the meaning of the word red giant by which
time
the moon will spiral into the earth and – this is the fun bit –
they will both fall fall fall
into the sun: star-crossed lovers united at last

I am writing to tell you this
black ink on moonstone
white chalk on lunar rock
look up

Rain and Deception

I pretend that all I want is to guide
the traffic of food in the right direction:
towards the mouth of the baby.
Meanwhile the sky
pretends there is a message
for me in its opulent drizzle.

Personally I prefer skies that pretend
to be painters.

I am not fooled and I certainly will not
endanger the silence
that lets me procrastinate
everything
not related to shovelling food
into this one hungry mouth.

I know the price of lying to yourself
is nothing to sneeze at.

it's never one of the good ones

where is my fucking palace?
where is my blood moon magic
& my ocean of nacreous ivory?

the only thing I am
allowed to carry
from my dream world into this one
is the nightmare:

10.000 newly hatched chicklets
chirping on a conveyor belt
carouseling towards
their premature deaths
they still cock their heads
(like all children)
their blameless primordial eyes
shining

The Clockmaker's Daughter

I never knew my mother
almost dropped out of clockmaking school
when she had to admit to herself
that there was something tick-ticking inside her:
something she had made not by squinting
through microscopes and careful attention to detail but instead
by neglect and forgetfulness (qualities they do not encourage
at the horological institute)
foxing her tutors with flowy dresses and ponchos
she stayed on and half a year later gave birth
to me right on the due date because
I was always going to be a punctual baby

and the first time she saw my round flat face
she smiled with relief: she knew just how to read me
she hummed along to the song of my cogs and gears
as she carried me into her workshop then
propped me against the wall between her assortment
of die plates and steel files and calipers
she worked late into the night furbishing my most important parts
with a small bow-lathe until she had polished me into
something she would not be ashamed to hand in as her
final assignment: an elaborate device with a steady heartbeat
the kind a room would feel empty without
a freestanding marvel with two hands and a mouth
for telling the truth of time

Sehnsucht

It's funny, you know:
somehow I do not miss you at all.

I sleep alone now and my dreams
are so much wilder
and my bed is so much wider
there's a forest by my headboard
and instead of crashing waves of cars
songbirds enchant me.

And the men here are boys
with tousled hair and tea-steeped voices
all gentle or coy or humble or rather
self-deprecating: if you cut them
they would bleed
banter they would
slash themselves open
to make me giggle or frown and I find the dance
of their teasing tongues more beautiful
even than birdsong.

And there is a garden here
that doesn't need watering.
Can you imagine
what it's like for me in a place
where the skies do more crying than I do
where everything runs on repressed passions
and irony and wanton
excessive apologies?

You see:
I no longer think of you at all

purple sea

the postal ship has come to the island
as it comes every week to bring the long-awaited mail

the pretty boy blushes as he reaches out for his letter
neither shouts nor taunts distract him

as he excavates the glass words of the one
he trusts will one day take him away

he smiles as he tries to think up replies in his mind
pearls are the birds that turned into your eyes

but before he can put them in writing a certain song
rises up from the sea interrupts with a lure he will not even try

to resist he will follow the siren call of scales and skin he will not
fight the fins teeth and fingers that await him beneath the waves

of quickly reddening blue

zombie apocalypse self-knowledge

well first of all you should not have to choose your lovers based on whether you think you'd survive a zombie apocalypse with them what if it never comes you say but what if it does come & what if you eat all of our carefully rationed mars bars at once & use the entire month's water supply for a bubble bath & we starve and also die of thirst & then you forget to lock up the back door and the zombies come streaming in one after the other slowly but surely like feral posh aunts & we can't even defend ourselves because you also used up all of our baseball bats for fire wood instead of layering up with more jumpers against the cold?

but I think you've got it all wrong you say in a zombie movie who survives ask yourself is it the one with the pre-numbered well-organised mars bars & spreadsheets or is it not maybe the one we are secretly rooting for (the anarchic bubble bath addicted hedonist entirely lacking in self-control?)

**concerning things which turn out to have an unexpected
application wholly different from their intended use**

the truth is that hope // was never meant to be this // sharp-boned
featherless bundle huddling // outside by the bins in the dark

someone once told you it was meant to be // a creature of awe //
a thing you would see from below // against an unknowable sky //
soaring // circling // its call as piercing as kite-song

and touch used to be how we mapped // our loves by // our bodies //
a gift // of gentleness now it is said // it's a silent weapon //
people used to // be harder to kill

once upon a time a curve // was our world's pleasantest shape //
a hillside // a dance // a blush // a bend and swell // now it's a
fault line // we try to flatten with solitude

false advertising*

reading this poem will make you the kind of person mirrors
smile at approvingly a person who doesn't look at the world
through a lens of survival but floats a little above their own sorrow

after you've devoured this poem you will understand
the animals even tree saplings
will follow you and sleep curled in your lap if you let them

small children will wave at you from car windows
strangers will offer you things you might need unprompted
like chocolates or answers or just a seat on a crowded train

your shoulders will unknot themselves
your most mind-numbing moments will charge up with wonder
your bedroom will turn a golden green forest grove replete with birdsong

after you've shared this poem everybody you love will not
only remember your birthday but also give you a gift
you have yearned for but did not know you deserved

oh and the person you've secretly loved all these years
will suddenly sit on your doorstep one day and smile up at you
with a slightly raised eyebrow that makes your breath catch

look I'm not kidding around here this poem will make you
beautiful this poem will make you special yes yes special and happy
and yes this poem will make you good

*(*the question is not whether any of this is true - the question is:
what if it is?)*

II   A FLIGHT OF FAMILIARS

Initiation

It starts with an apple –
not poisoned, nothing so ordinary.
Just a round ruddy marvel grown from bitter
seeds – the lush daughter of time and the patience
of trees.

Pick the apple that calls to you. You cannot go wrong.
She will have picked you in her turn. Hold her
close to your face. Seek your own
reflection in her red. Bite down. Isolate
the edge of her acerbity from the sweetness until you find
the sting: a sour prickle, but not unpleasant.
Swallow.

Now let the wish rise. You thought you knew it, you don't.
You thought it was yours, yet you'd never understood that you'd
been sheltering
such yearning, unfamiliar in its sudden force.
Let it fill you, but don't hold it, let it go without speaking.
Unleash it with a quiet breath, palms open.
(You will need to uncurl your fists for this.)

What leaves you is more than a wind storm or even a creature.
It is something you made but cannot comprehend.
When you have recovered from the shock,
the frightening jolt and scope of your power,
you coil back into yourself, stilled.
Like the quiet mother of a wilful child you watch it whirl and
rage and tear
at the fabric of the world.
You stand there as a sapling might, calm
within your new-found emptiness,
and tell yourself the unfamiliar truth
that you are ready –

Colour of the Witch

I have yet to see an ugly tree –
it is not even your line but he smiles lips curled
around his silence as they sometimes curve
around his vowels you can tell even though
he is walking ahead because he is holding
your hand

stay away from the boy they'd said
we hear that emerald's his favourite colour
keep away from the boy they'd said
for willows are his favourite trees

it is true that his words are like falling
through forest floor
his voice like the soft ground
you wish to be buried in
other men have tried to gain your heart
with cash or songs or poetry
all it took for him to break you was what?
one glance through his colourless lashes
one shrug half a name

stay away from the boy they'd said
we hear that emerald's his favourite colour
keep away from the boy they'd said *for*
willows are his favourite trees

& it is true
that after the first time he kissed you
he left you alone in a clearing
& when you stood there
fist raised against the sky
a sparrow hawk shot down to land on your hand
gave you a long inscrutable stare
then flew off again

(your mother noticed you
shaking at dinner that night)

stay away from the boy they'd said
we hear that emerald's his favourite colour
keep away from the boy they'd said *for*
willows are his favourite trees

& it is true that all night
grows heavier, darker around him
the wind louder
its song more pronounced
and that after the first time he murmured
I love you
& left you half-naked and giddy
behind the woodshed
you found you were suddenly able to dictate
the movements of clouds with your mind

stay away from the boy they'd said
we hear that emerald's his favourite colour
keep away from the boy they'd said *for*
willows are his favourite trees

& while their warning words are nothing to you it is
also true that his leaf-like fingers are curled around
the seeds of all sorrow all sadness all pain not just
yours or his – everyone's
he might plant a new seedling
every once in a while
but for now he is only walking ahead
for now he is holding your hand

familiar

I knew you for what you were the second
you stepped in the garden I knew you
at first glance

not by the absence
of a tame crow nestled
against your wind hair

nor by the way you shied from the reverend's
hosepipe even the tiniest
splash of his water

not by your sober green dress
nor your cultured manner of speaking
and holding your head just so:

I knew you by my own blood
the way a planet knows her moons
or a cloud knows her nascent lightning

Medusae

Do not lose faith on the day you wake up
with spiders instead of hair.
Do not cry as you look in the mirror.
Remember: They may stay. They may not.
They are here for now.
If you must, take pains to cover your head.
Hide their crawling under your most elegant hat
lest people recoil from you in the streets.
Or don't. Remember Medusa and her snakes.
She'd turn anyone to stone if they looked at her frightened.
She was a monster and proud. All hiss, curse and scorn: danger.

And yet to think someone must have loved her enough
to name half of all jellyfish
those moon-glowing blooms of floating
fluorescent umbrellas and bells
after her.

for soft long ears

she says my mare is quiet

they say affection is inconceivable and dim
they say possessions are sombre and vile
they give dark speeches in between mouthfuls of cake

she says not your mare but mine

they say each moment knows only how to
separate death from sharper death
they say bad ideas are shadow flowers

she says my mare is a fleck-coated fact

they say then why not kiss every little colt forlorn
all those lost ones between steed and stallion
they tell her to truly dance is to give something away

she says my mare is not a trinket

she says if you listen
the listening outlives
our dreadful language

26

Storm Petrel (Pitt Rivers Museum, case 29a)

Oh take your pity elsewhere,
landlocked stranger,
I am still waiting to burn.

Yes, I was the soul bird
of a dozen drowned sailors,
was wave-walker, weathervane,
Black Mary's chicklet,
harbinger of stormy seas,
pelagic stow-away.

They feared me,
called me satanita,
water-witch.

I was meant to end at the hand of men
who know that one
tarred string
is enough to tell the bird
from the candle,
the witch from the flame.

But take your sad eyes elsewhere,
stranger, listen –
one day the storm will find me,
and I'll blaze.

tiny choirboy

for Rose and her son Theo

we came in from the dark & on our night-time walk we had seen
so many spooky black trees that ghosts seemed a real possibility

(that's when I first saw you)

surrounded by figures in white robes - eidolons maybe, slowly advancing,
beckoning us into the candle light, you led the way and we followed
in silence: our trust rewarded in the gold of a cold college chapel filled
with evensong from a dozen throats & I saw your earnest face aglow
with concentration - saw it disappear as you sat down –
that's how tiny you were

(and my life was yours)

you see something about your innocent joy as you joined in with
the angelical song in such a secret, mysterious place had reminded me
with bewildering force of someone, someone…

(my unborn son)

advice from one who's been burnt before

on the first day the dragon moves in
don't tell the neighbours but
take the batteries out of your smoke detector
you'll thank me later
you can stop paying your electricity bills
even asleep a dragon is more
than a room-full of candles

if you are stumped for what to feed your dragon a
little fire goes a long way
buy a multipack of tea lights
fire is what it breathes & what burns in its veins
it's also what it likes to snack on every once in a while
the way bees love to eat
honey but also make honey

oh and most important of all
if your dragon is thirsty give it verses but no water
never water but maybe a song if it is scared stroke its
wings till your hand scorches
or let it listen to the ember bloom rhythm of slow
soft breathing that rises from you like smoke
as you drift off in its glow

Saying Goodbye to Wychwood
for Léonie and Rosie

I've never had an easy time
letting go: I let places I love
seep into my bloodstream and I have hurt
myself this way before.

Remember the dog was in love
with these carpets, was never
happier than flying through wheat fields
with her long bat ears for wings.

Here's where we learned about warmth
and the furtive language of
wisteria, where I found out there are mothers here
who let you come as you are.

The country walks made me feel written.
Deer in a flower field,
a lonely oak in its own autumn halo,
the shock of a dead baby rabbit.

Sheep eying my whereabouts
with suspicion, sheep grilling me
on my intentions
in their peeved human voices.

And on my boots, on my dress,
dozens of burrs hitching rides,
clustering onto me and each other
like small brown barnacles.

I've never understood them
more than today.
I too want nothing
but this:

to burrow into a place undetected,
sink my velcro hooks into its fabric
and hold on, hold on as if
I'd never let go.

Aurae

for Lucy and Sophia

The men that came for our gold found no fire,
nor even the memory of fire.

The men that came for our gold found no gold,
nor even the idea of gold.

They found four quiet sisters
in a winter-cold house.

Four still girls shrugging, smiling as if to say take
what you will, but as you see there is nothing to take.

As soon as they left we resumed our singing
and the fire blazed up in the grate.

The men that came for our gold talked like fools,
blind with a story of treasure.

They did not know what was hidden
deep, glinting: that our gold was song.

Raising Astaroth

I sang you into our lives with three secret words
from a spell-book I sang you lullabies backwards I
wept as you rose from the flame

you are not my flesh not my blood you are my child
so what if your milk is raw meat
and your day is my night and your kiss is all teeth

my nephews and nieces do not call you their cousin
if you ever met them for play they would run from you crying
and horrified
with your claw-marks red on their well-meaning hands

for all intents and purposes we are your family until your last
sulphur breath
and we will live to give you all we can give
even if friends turn on the threshold and we are no longer welcome
at parties

I pretend I don't sense some unspoken wish for a real human child
sometimes they bring up adoption in a hushed voice
so as not to alarm you

for all intents and purposes you are a child who will never grow up
a child
that never once said the words I'm hungry Mummy all you ever
say is I love you
I love you in all the ways you can think of over and over

and I will never tire of it although this is a love I know
is going to kill me
my fanged angel

anemochory

as soon as the light fades
and dusk threatens darkness
there is no antidote
to the poison of waiting

so put on your coat
go outside and keep walking
until you have found the expanse of
a dandelion field

where the rough winds and rain
have left the soft puffs
a little bedraggled
wet white manes hanging off drooping stalks

it may take a little more skill
to extract a wish from these specimens
you will have to blow a little harder
to scatter your request

you may need a little more courage to
entrust your desire to these humble
emissaries in the gloaming
but what choice do you have

aftermath

as the moon
flares up silver

*(somehow I am still
here)*

around the clouds'
crumpled edges

*(somehow I am still
here)*

a young fox zooms
across the park knowing
the bins are mostly hers
after closing time
if she learns to contend with
the magpies and crows

*(somehow I am still here
still holding on to
a melancholy milk
thistle stalk as if
it were a life line
which tethers us all)*

III   **HOSTINGHOSTING**

prediction

they will not come for us
as long as we stand here
with our faces turned
towards the bleeding blue
unblinking:

as long as we keep clutching
these tree trunks
breathing only
towards tomorrow
they will not come for us

but once we pick up our bag shrug
them off and start walking
(me like someone with a purpose
you like someone who
could not conceive
of such a thing
as a backwards glance)

they will come
and they will be
too late

What It Felt Like

Here's some questions I consider safe
and appropriate topics for conversation:
You could ask me about that island of plastic debris floating in the ocean
and how many days you might need to walk across without
getting from one end to the other.
       (Seven, it's seven.)
You might ask me about my family,
growing up as the youngest of five.
        (Gets away with murder, that little urchin,
         everyone used to say.)
Or ask me about my favourite sound.
         (It is this: the soft click of my front door closing on the
         last caller,
         the empty house singing to itself, the almost-silence.)

But please do not ask what it felt like.
I will have no answer for you except please
do not ever ask me this question again.
I will even pretend to cry at first so you do not press on
with this line of inquiry; and then cry for real.
I won't know where the switch happens.
I don't know if I owe you an answer.
When or how I should stop sobbing.
Because what is a long enough time to fend off such a query?
A minute, a day?
         (Or, hey, seeing as the floodgates are open
         might as well cry on till Michaelmas?)
What do you want to know?
If it severed my soul into two broken parts?
If I regret it?
         (If I regret it!)

(Look, I cannot tell you what it felt like
in the moment. The memory is grainy at best,
and wordless.
            (But I can tell you this
            because it is simpler:
            I am glad, monstrous glad, I am ecstatic
            that he is dead, and I alive;
            not the other way around.)

adaptation

I've adapted well to the new situation
I say it and in the telling realize it's a little lie

because that is not quite what happened
I did not need to make an adjustment

there have not been any changes
I had already learned to keep strangers at bay

two meters or more at all times
I was already familiar with the cold sinking

feeling from reading the news
and the fact that it suddenly concerns you

I was already living a slow life
that might end in a bad way

already hoarding tins like armour for an uncertain future I already had
days I lived under the duvet and saw no human faces

I was already expert at simmering in low-level dread
like black bath water

so what I should have said was
the situation has very well adapted to me

On Working In A Shop

Cycling to work along the towpath
by the river to the sound of my crumbling
bike's creaking - I notice the willows
have turned their long hair auburn.

I suppose this marks the beginning
of autumn, which must mean that I have been
working in the same job in the same shop
for over a year now.

What have I learned? That the soul
is resilient. It will refuse to be crushed
by tedium. Instead it will latch
onto little delights; and thrive.

For while I take no particular pleasure
in the mopping and vacuuming, the dusting,
smiling, serving, being paid for politeness, there is one
task in my workday that makes my bored heart soar:

Holding a sharp pocket knife, I slice open boxes
finding the catch between two flaps of cardboard I sever
their brown tape like tendons and out
spill their contents: a perpetual Christmas.

In another life I might have been a butcher,
a hunter or fisher, maybe an assassin…
But in this one I wield my little knife
disembowelling boxes, almost content.

what we know

I.

that you are writing this outside by the light of the moss pink moon
(egg moon)
& that what we are trying to achieve here are happy endings
– for once

many people don't believe in them – but then again many people
don't believe
in a lot of things (moon baths – for one)

II.

that headlines referring to pink super moons
will never fail to tickle you though the why of it is hard to explain

III.

that you are trying to think which adventures or misadventures could befall
someone staying at home in their tower or hovel or palace – the small

patch of garden they live on – the island they got banished to
for being too good at spells

& what kind of escapades are there to be had short of waiting around
for visiting dragons or couriers or – you shudder to think – questing heroes?

the kinds that require a pencil – a miniscule notebook – a very bright moon
& some scribbling – also wearing a fairy tale night gown & drinking

bay leaf & rose tea for the very first time in your life
(you could plant your hands into the dirt or your nose on one of the cherry

blossoms you have waited five years for)
or you could say what you wish for out loud in the night

say it now – the secret is – *fulfilled dreams will always birth more dreams*
& you will have to be quick before your daughter calls you back
into the house

& scolds you for being out at this hour wearing only your nightie
are you trying to catch your death she will say with loving
exasperation so speak

the words you came here to say– they are less
of a wish & really more of a thank-you

then grab your mug & your notebook & pencil
& follow the call back inside

where the fire is lit & each bedroom awaits
the quiet song of a dreaming sleeper

IV.

that what you know as this moment =
what we are going to rename as
once upon a time

but the dancer

makes herself
out of yielding dead
wood and maybe a garbled
lyric floating by
tuneless still almost a song

she cups the length of her leg
in her own hands
a bid to piece new bits of herself together
she is not over she may be tattered
yet she is unbounded

she is eternal
takes flight half-finished
exalts in her movements
she'll pay with her pain or
whatever it takes

her measures erode any unhelpful sense of
which way is up, up or sideways or down
she knows infinity she also knows
as long as bodies can break or be broken or bought
dreams can be flogged like spirits

but that's why
the dancer
the unbreakable dancer
makes
herself

to the man who told me my yellow bobble hat makes me look old

did you know there is an app that lets me see into the future (there is an app for almost anything these days) let me be more precise – this one lets me see the future of my face the simulation is so convincing I'm becoming a little bit obsessed with it a preview of my drooping skin my future double chin and my nose a huge gnarly potato tuber smack in the middle of everything the way my eyes will shrink and my lips thin out and turn into my mother's I spent my whole childhood waiting to grow up grow old enough grow into this life that lets me eat cake with whipped cream for breakfast and walk my dog but I notice how the days are getting shorter now and more lonely I don't get my ID checked in supermarkets or bars any more also I am still very scared of everything almost all of the time I'm getting worse at moving my body though space (though I'm still good at daydreams) so this is how I spend my short lonely nights I take pictures and pictures of my face with my phone's selfie cam then with one easy click I age them about thirty years I recommend this as a hobby - I'm getting used to my future self (it's the projected wrinkles I like the most) I know her so well now that sometimes when I look at myself I see her waiting behind my crumbly façade sometimes she is half of a story book sorceress half my own Turkish grandma the latter when she seems as if she has laughed a lot and bakes chocolate biscuits for all the kids on her road and you know what? I cannot wait to be this old crone I bet she doesn't bother with those witch hairs that sprout in threes from her chin or the plucking of eyebrows I bet she still loves banana splits as much as I do I bet she still rereads the first books she owned with her bespectacled eyes in a squint I bet she has too many dogs and not enough sense I bet she kept the yellow bobble hat I'm wearing right now in a drawer with some mothballs I really hope I will get to meet her face in the mirror one day: so familiar I've already begun loving it

There's A Tyre Swing In Bagley Wood

a first line is not a poem
a punctured secret is not a poem

that dog turd you picked up with a big shard
of glass: not a poem

the fact that the bird you love best
is a mistle thrush

whose song is always in
a minor key

though delightful
is still not a poem

nor is loneliness
nor is oblivion

the tyre swing in bagley wood
is a tyre swing – not a poem

the realization that right now there are more poets alive
than dead in the past is – you guessed it – not quite a poem

the stranger who thought that life
looks like a dreadful path

that nevertheless
we can walk it

that the powers we carry are nameless
until we are forced to call on them

was most likely a poet
which still does not make their reflections a poem

so what is a poem?
what is a poem?

is only a question ever a poem? do mistle thrushes sing
in a minor key?

are they really your favourite birds?
are you lonely? how lonely?

have you ever been down to bagley wood?
I haven't

my entire bagley wood knowledge is
hearsay

is there a tyre swing in bagley wood?

hostinghosting

a)

those that lasted   kiss goodbye
let them arrive greet you   then slip away

this is the miracle of   youth
being able to give things   to the dead
with their enchanted   tears your

selves your eyes or just   infinity
whichever closed-off treasures   the lost
souls are   seeking

b)

this white four-poster once
was her laughter & the darkening

night sky once was her tongue
the orangery once was a little

tear she showed no one isn't it striking
these shooting stars were

how she sneezed when
the dust came down the cashmere

I'm wearing once was her left
foot this Jasmine bush here used to be

the way she tilted her head
when not really listening those peacocks

once were her elbows the twin
dolls her headaches oh and I think

this stuffed swan was actually her heart
once but this whole country used to be

her heart come to think of it
all the cliffs & wild springs & lava fields

the unending summers the northern lights
jade flames against a black canvas

salt apples

unable to sleep
amid all the salt and the racket
(sleep belongs to the dead)
even the rose-coloured apples
are carnival-starved
(sadness is a prerequisite for
dancing) like grape-fuelled
lightning *(like winter*
may wait)

nothing perishes nothing persists the ceiling
swirls in a red maze
I eat and hold hands over my billowing dress
couples slouch off together
pale little ones and big ones in heavy colours a
rasping chill of voices that circle and dive *(thank*
you for smashing it — and thank me too!)

during my levity moths and moments die and slink away
no one speaks the unbreakable word
no

while I say nothing
morning lights itself

Acknowledgments

'adaptation': with gratitude to *Wingless Dreamer* and the *Project Lockdown Anthology.*

'advice from one who's been burnt before': with gratitude to Mona Arshi and the *2020 Live Canon Anthology.*

'aftermath': with gratitude to *Parkinson's Poetry Competition.*

'but the dancer': with gratitude to *Visual Verse.*

'concerning things...': with gratitude to Anna Saunders and the *2020 Wirral Poetry Festival Open Poetry Competition.*

'false advertising': with gratitude to Paul McGrane and the '*What The Moon Was Told'* anthology of the Brian Dempsey Memorial Pamphlet Prize.

'for soft long ears': with gratitude to *Animal.*

'hostinghosting b)': with gratitude to Nancy Mattson, Michael Bartholomew-Briggs, and the 2020 *Acumen Poetry Competition* (under the title 'All That is Left of Liv')

'insomnia': with gratitude to *Frozen Wavelets.*

'Initiation': with gratitude to the *Magic* anthology by the Gloucestershire Poetry Society.

'never one of the good ones': with gratitude to *Rise Up Review.*

'On Working In A Shop': with gratitude to the *Yeovil Prize* and *harana.*

'prediction': with gratitude to *The Voices Project Poetry Library.*

'salt apples': with gratitude to *Lucent Dreaming.*

'Sehnsucht': with gratitude to Zaffar Kunial and the *2019 Live Canon Anthology.*

'Storm Petrel': with gratitude to *Whirlagust*, the *Yaffle Prize Anthology;* and *Tiny Seed Journal.*

'The Clockmaker's Daughter': with gratitude to Liz Berry and the *2018 Live Canon Anthology;* and *Tales from the Forest.*

'There's A Tyre Swing In Bagley Wood': with gratitude to Matt Bryden and the 2020 Charroux Prize.

'tiny choirboy': with gratitude to Paul Sutherland and the '*PRECIOUS'* Hammond House Poetry Prize Anthology.

'What It Felt Like': with gratitude to Jackie Kay and the *2019 Oxford Brookes Poetry Prize.*

'writer in residence': with gratitude to *Abyss & Apex.*

'zombie apocalypse self-knowledge': with gratitude to *Dreams & Nightmares.*

Thank you ...

To start off my thank-yous, I am going to borrow the words of Ada Limon: "We write with all the good ghosts in our corners. I, for one, have never made anything alone, never written a single poem alone..." There are so many wondrous good ghosts that I owe these poems to.

First of all, my most heartfelt thanks to my fantastic, supportive, generous and patient publishers Janice and Dónall and also the wonderful Paul McGrane for selecting me for the Brian Dempsey Memorial Pamphlet Award and magically making this little book a reality.

To my family, my open-hearted parents and the best sisters in the universe: Thank you for believing in my crazy career in writing and always supporting my dreams.

To Rowena, who is a poetry wizard and genius. Thanks for teaching me so much and making this a better book.

To Rose and MK, thank you so much for all your priceless feedback, cheering-on, and hand-holding – I am so glad we have each other's backs. You're the best.

To Phoebe, the Oxford Poetry Library and the LIT Poetry Group: Thank you for giving me a safe space to create and share some of these poems for the very first time while I was finding my poetry wings again.

Many of these poems exist only because of Lucy and Sophia, Mesendorf, and also William and all the incredible Duggans' Decameronians, who delighted and inspired and kept me sane during this year's lockdown: Thank you so much for everything, especially all the brilliant prompts!
And a second thank-you to the phenomenal Sophia for our joint project *10 years – words & question marks,* let's do a follow-up soon, I will always be your biggest fan :)

The writing legends Daisy, Matt, Kiran, Tom, Sarvat, Lucy, Paul and Jessie, thank you for the 100-day writing challenge and all the inspiration and incredible generosity and kindness.

Clare and Leonie, words cannot describe how much our times together have meant to me. I hope we'll have the chance of many more retreats and sourdough brunches and fireside chats.

Thank you to the magical Catweazle Community, I miss you.

The Poetry and Pancakes crew and the Storytellers' Supper Club. Thanks so, so much for filling this strange year with beautiful words.

Infinite gratitude to everyone who offered help with the cover picture, but especially Rosie, Deano, and Alev.

Sophie and the Writing Habit. Claire, Ditte, Vicky. Hannah, James, Calum, Sam N. and Sam D. Klaus, Steffi & Emil. Fab. So much gratitude to all of you. And Rosie one more time, a billion more times.

I would also like to thank all the editors of the magazines and anthologies and competitions that first published some of these poems – thank you for the awe-inspiring work you do.

My gratitude to my fellow writers in the MSt Creative Writing cohorts and all the writing tutors who ever taught me. Special thanks to Jane Draycott who taught me about turning poems upside down and Jamie McKendrick who first taught me the magic of making up poetry translations from unfamiliar languages - I sneaked many of those into this book…

Last but not least to Nick, who has patiently put up with my poetry efforts for more than half of his life and once wrote me a sonnet comparing my face to a schnitzel. And of course my little daemon dog for being a reluctant muse and for always closing my laptop with her paw if I attempt to read her any of my poetry. I named her after a writer who is very good at making fun of poets, so it's no less than I deserve.

About Laura Theis

Laura Theis grew up in Germany, moved to the UK a decade ago, and writes poems, stories and songs, in her second language.

She has an MSt (Distinction) in Creative Writing from Keble College, Oxford.

Her work has been published in the UK, Ireland, Belgium, Germany, Canada and the U.S.

An *AM Heath Prize* recipient, she has also won the *Brian Dempsey Memorial Pamphlet Prize*, the *Hammond House International Literary Award for Poetry,* and the 2020 *Mogford Short Story Prize.* She was runner-up for the *Mslexia Flash Fiction Prize* and a finalist in over twenty other international poetry and fiction competitions including the *Poetry International Prize* and the *Cambridge Prize.*

The poems in this collection have won or been shortlisted for the *Acumen Poetry Prize,* the *Geoff Stevens Memorial Poetry Prize,* three consecutive *Live Canon International Poetry Awards,* the *Hammond House Award,* the *Yeovil Prize,* the *Wirral Poetry Festival Competition,* the *Blue Nib Chapbook Contest,* the *Yaffle Prize,* the *Charroux Prize,* and the *Oxford Brookes Poetry Prize* judged by Jackie Kay.

Laura's work has also been widely anthologised and appears in a variety of literary journals including *Mslexia, Strange Horizons, Abyss&Apex, harana, The London Reader,* and *Rise Up Review.*

This is her very first (and, so far, best!) book of poetry.